PICTURE THIS

FUN PHOTOGRAPHY AND CRAFTS

Debra Friedman

KIDS CAN PRESS

For the boys — Bob, Nathan, Joseph and Eli

Text © 2003 Debra Friedman
Illustrations © 2003 Kids Can Press

KIDS CAN DO IT and the 📷 logo are trademarks of Kids Can Press Ltd.

Kids Can Press acknowledges the financial support of the Government of Canada, through the BPIDP, for our publishing activity.

Published in Canada by
Kids Can Press Ltd.
29 Birch Avenue
Toronto, ON M4V 1E2

Published in the U.S. by
Kids Can Press Ltd.
2250 Military Road
Tonawanda, NY 14150

www.kidscanpress.com

Edited by Kat Mototsune
Designed by Karen Powers
Cover photo by Ray Boudreau
Printed in Hong Kong, China, by Wing King Tong Company Limited

The hardcover edition of this book is smyth sewn casebound.
The paperback edition of this book is limp sewn with a drawn-on cover.

CM 03 0 9 8 7 6 5 4 3 2 1
CM PA 03 0 9 8 7 6 5 4 3 2 1

National Library of Canada Cataloguing in Publication Data

Friedman, Debra (Debra Lynne), 1955–

    Picture this : fun photography and crafts / written by Debra Friedman ; illustrated by Jane Kurisu.

(Kids can do it)

ISBN 1-55337-046-5 (bound).
ISBN 1-55337-047-3 (pbk.)

1. Photography — Juvenile literature. 2. Handicraft — Juvenile literature. I. Kurisu, Jane II. Title. III. Series.

TR149.F75 2003   j770   C2002-902207-X

Photo credits

Abbreviations
t = top; b = bottom; c = center; l = left; r = right

Title Page: Meichan Waxer; **p. 10**: Christopher Lue; **p. 11**: Christopher Lue; **p. 15**: Zoe Lawlor-Hill; **p. 16**: Zoe Lawlor-Hill; **p. 17**: Zoe Lawlor-Hill; **p. 19**: Jim Paterson; **p. 20**: Jim Paterson; **p. 21**: Jim Paterson; **p. 25**: Sidney Hederitch; **p. 26**: Jaime Maddalena; **p. 27**: Jaime Maddalena; **p. 28**: Phil Taylor (b); **p. 29**: Jennifer Long (l); **p. 29**: Meichan Waxer (r); **p. 30**: Meichan Waxer; **p. 32**: Jennifer Griffiths (t); **p. 33**: Nelson Manuel; **p. 36**: Karen Chapelle (t, r); Cathy Bidini (b, r); Bob Walsh (t, l); Cathy Bidini (b, l); **p. 37**: Alex Hickox; **p. 38**: Jaime Maddalena. All other photos by Debra Friedman.

Thanks to models: Emma, Samantha, Katie, Arthur, Charlie, Morgan, Zack, Hannah, and Mona

Thanks to Johnnie Eisen, Jay Teitel, Susan Ross, and Bob Burley for advice

Kids Can Press is a *Corus*™ Entertainment Company

Contents

Introduction

Think about how many times you've had your picture taken. Photography is a great way to keep memories, but that's only the beginning of what you can do with a camera. Just look around you to discover a world of exciting images. In this book you'll find some wild ways to take photos of things and people you see every day.

Once you've taken a picture, what do you do with it? This book will show you some great things to make with your photos once you've had them developed. Have fun and remember: cameras don't take pictures — people do. Go ahead — shoot!

How to Hold Your Camera

Any of these poses will help you keep your camera steady. Crouching or lying on your stomach will let you see things from a different angle.

Your Camera

There are lots of kinds of cameras available, but you can do everything in this book with a "point and shoot" 35 mm snapshot camera. Whether you use that, a one-use disposable camera or a digital camera, make sure you read the camera's manual or the package instructions first.

Shutter release – *the button you push to take the photo by moving the shutter, the curtain inside the camera that lets in light*

Viewfinder – *the window you look through*

Flash – *the light in your camera to use when there is not enough light to take a clear photo. (Keep turned off when taking most pictures in this book.)*

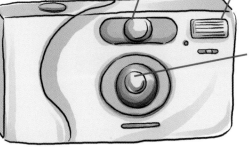

Lens – *the piece of glass or plastic where the light enters the camera*

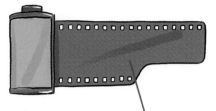 

Film – *to check if a roll of film has been used, look at the cassette.*

Before the film is used, some film will hang out.

After the pictures are taken and the film is rewound, no film will show.

Film Facts

You can take all the photos in this book in about 50 shots. Here are some tips on the film you need:

● Two rolls of 24-shot film or two 27-shot one-use cameras should do it.

● Use film marked "daylight" for outdoor pictures.

● Use 35 mm film with a speed of 200 or 400 marked on the box. You can use one roll of each, starting with 400 if you work through this book in order.

● Any of the photos in this book can be taken with either color or black-and-white film. Black-and-white film may be harder to find and have developed, but can give you some neat effects.

 All film has a number that shows how fast, or light-sensitive, it is. Faster film has a higher number (400+). That means you need less light to take a picture.

Drawing with Light

The word photograph means "drawing with light." When this photo was taken, light came through the window, went into the camera lens and shone on the film. Where the kid blocked the light from hitting the film, a silhouette, or outline, was formed. With a camera, you do the "drawing" — you don't just *take* the pictures, you *make* the pictures to show other people how you see the world.

For great results, remember these tips every time you take a picture:

● **Subject:** Make sure you are close enough to whatever you are taking a photo of.

● **Light:** Check the film package for what kind of light conditions you need to make a good photo.

● **Composition:** If it looks too busy inside the viewfinder, move the camera around until the shot is simpler.

● **Angle:** Before you shoot, get higher or lower than your subject to see how it looks from a different angle.

● **Focus:** Look at your subject from up close and far away. If you are too close (check manual or instructions), your subject might be out of focus. You may like this effect — or you may not.

● **Permission:** Get permission before you take photos of people or photograph on private property.

☞ Try This　Fun Photogram

You can draw with light without a camera by making a photogram. Try this on a sunny day.

1. Put a sheet of construction paper on a cookie sheet.

2. Find objects with definite shapes — flowers and leaves, toys or the tools you used for a construction project. Put them on the construction paper. Make sure the objects don't overlap. If it is windy, tape down the objects or place a piece of glass over them.

3. Leave the paper in the sunny spot. If the sun moves, move the cookie sheet so your photogram is in the sun. Start with two hours. The sun will fade the part of the paper not covered by the objects.

4. Check your photogram by carefully lifting an object and having a peek. The longer the sun shines on it, the more difference there will be between the faded paper and the covered parts. If the paper hasn't faded enough, replace the objects and leave your photogram out for another hour or so.

5. Once your images are as dark as you like, remove the objects and take the paper out of the light.

6. If you want your photogram to last, photocopy it. If you don't, you'll see the light keep fading the paper until the images fade away.

A digital camera captures your picture as little rectangles called pixels — short for "picture elements" — that are saved in a digital file instead of on film.

Window Matte Frame

Every photograph needs three things. First, there's the photographer — that's you! Next, you need a subject, the thing you take the picture of. The third thing is whoever sees the photo once it's developed. When this picture was taken, the photographer wanted to show something that would surprise the viewers — how long is that kid?! When you make a frame for your photographs, it helps you say, "Hey! Look at this!"

You will need

- any photo 10 cm x 15 cm (4 in. x 6 in.)
- a piece of construction paper 20 cm x 25 cm (8 in. x 10 in.)
- a piece of corrugated cardboard (optional)
- a piece of thin cardboard or bristol board 20 cm x 25 cm (8 in. x 10 in.)
- a pencil, a ruler, sharp scissors or an X-Acto knife, tape or double-sided tape, glue

1 Lay your photo right side up on the construction paper. Move the photo until the borders around the picture look right to you. You may want to make the bottom border bigger than the top.

2 Trace around your picture with the pencil. Remove the picture. This side is the back of your matte.

3 Using the ruler, measure and draw another set of lines 0.5 cm (¼ in.) inside the traced lines.

5 Tape your photo face down to the back of the matte so the picture shows through.

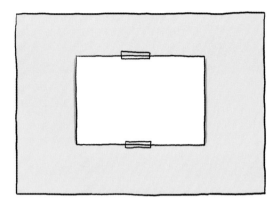

4 Carefully poke the scissors into the middle of the paper, then cut along the inside lines. Or ask an adult to help you cut using the knife and ruler. If you use the X-Acto knife, cut on the corrugated cardboard to protect your work surface.

6 Glue the back of the photo and the frame to the thin cardboard.

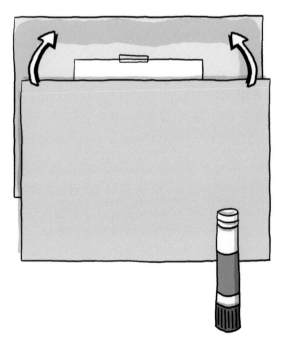

Light and Shadow

You need light to make a photograph, but that's not all light can do. It can make a photo seem happy or sad, realistic or dreamy. It can be natural, like in this picture, or artificial. It can light up every corner or cast long shadows like the ones you see here.

How does this picture make you feel? The shadow of the clock on the sidewalk is a surprise — showing a familiar thing in an unexpected place is a great way to get the viewer's attention. The dark areas make the photograph feel mysterious. The contrast between the blurry shadow of the moving leg and the clear shadow of the still clock may make you think about time passing.

▶ Too much light coming into the camera will make the image look washed out, or overexposed, like the one here.

▶ If there's not enough light, the photo will be underexposed and too dark. This photo was taken with just the right amount of light.

Make the Photo

Go outside on a shadow hunt. Find two shadows that look interesting. Take one photo of each shadow and one photo of each thing casting the shadow.

● Look for objects with interesting shapes and strong outlines — the outline of something is called its silhouette.

● Don't just look on the ground — look at walls too.

● If you don't see interesting shadows, make them. Move things around or get someone to stand in different positions.

● Make sure your own shadow doesn't get in the way!

Think about including things in your photos that add information. In the picture of three girls (on the opposite page) did you notice the word "best" on the box? It was included to show that they are best friends — and the viewer doesn't need a caption to see that!

Shadow Frame

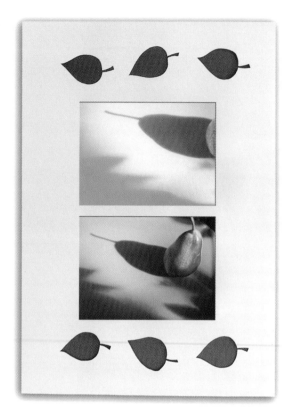

What better way to show off pictures of shadows than with a frame with shadow cutouts? This kind of double frame is called a diptych.

You will need

- 2 photos from Make the Photo on page 11 (a shadow and the object that cast it)
- a piece of white bristol board 27 cm x 35 cm (11 in. x 14 in.)
- a piece of corrugated cardboard
- a piece of black or gray bristol board 27 cm x 35 cm (11 in. x 14 in.)
- scissors, a ruler, a pencil, an X-Acto or utility knife, tape or double-sided tape, glue

1 Use scissors to cut away parts of the photos you don't want to show. (This is called cropping your photos.) Leave a 1 cm (½ in.) border around what you want to show.

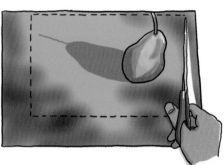

2 Position your cropped photos on the back of the white bristol board. Place them sideways or upside down if you like.

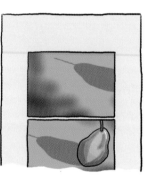

3 Trace around your pictures with the pencil. Remove the pictures. Measure and draw another set of lines 0.5 cm (¼ in.) inside the traced lines.

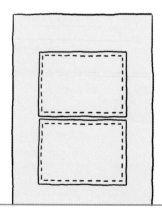

4 Place the white bristol board on the corrugated cardboard to protect your work surface. Ask an adult to help you cut along the inside lines using the X-Acto knife and ruler.

5 Draw shadow shapes around the holes. You can use the same shapes as the shadow in the photo, or different shapes.

6 With the corrugated cardboard still under the white bristol board, ask an adult to help you cut out the shadow shapes using the knife.

7 Tape the photos face-down to the side of the white bristol board with the pencil marks so the pictures show through.

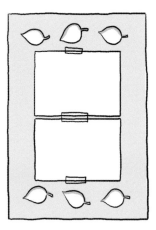

8 Glue the back of the photos and the white bristol board frame to the black bristol board. The black should show through the shapes cut out of the white bristol board.

Everyday Things

If you breathe on your camera lens, you can get an extraordinary image of an ordinary thing. Even laundry on the clothesline can seem magical. If you were going to shoot a whole roll of film in an hour, what would you shoot? There are so many things around you that could make good photos. Your pictures might show what life is like in your house, in your neighborhood — or even in your dreams! And you might be surprised at how some ordinary things, like a TV screen, look when they are photographed.

👉 Try This

Photographic Scavenger Hunt

Take five pictures of five everyday things. Here are a few ideas to get you started:

- your favorite meal
- your best friend holding a picture of herself
- your dad sleeping
- a TV set, turned on
- a person and his reflection in a puddle

Make the Photo

Did you know that letters of the alphabet can hide in everyday things? Go out and find the letters in your name. Take photos of the letter shapes.

● Take as many photos as there are letters in your name. If there are fewer than 10 letters, the rest can be pictures of things you see every day.

● If you get really stuck, use letters from signs, or write letters on the pavement with sidewalk chalk. You could even take a picture of a brick wall and color in the letters on the developed photo.

● Get close. Make the letters take up as much of the photo as possible.

 **Tech Talk**

Whatever is closest to the camera when you shoot will be in the foreground of your picture. Whatever is farther away will be in the background.

Star Nameplate

Be a star! Hang this sign on your bedroom door to let people know your name and what your everyday life is like.

You will need

- photos from Make the Photo on page 15
- a piece of heavy cardboard
- a piece of corrugated cardboard (optional)
- 2 small suction hooks
- colored markers, scissors, glue, an X-Acto or utility knife, a pencil, a hole punch

1 If the letters in your photos are hard to read, go over them with markers. Trim the photos if you like.

2 Draw a star shape on the cardboard. Arrange the photos on the cardboard so that they spell your name inside the star shape. Then arrange any other photos around your name inside the star shape. Glue the photos to the cardboard and let dry.

3 Ask an adult to help you cut along the star shape using the X-Acto knife. Cut on the corrugated cardboard to protect your work surface.

4 Depending on the shape of your sign you'll need to make one or two holes near the top. Ask an adult to help you make the holes.

5 Measure the distance between the holes in your nameplate. Mark spots on your door that distance apart and attach the suction hooks.

6 Hang your nameplate on the hooks.

Inside the Frame

The top, bottom and sides of every photograph make a frame. The frame includes everything you want in your picture and keeps out what you don't. When pictures are put together like this, they make a panorama. A panorama shows what goes on beyond the frame of a single photo.

Good composition — the way you plan your shot — makes a photograph easy and fun to look at. Separately, these photos (below) don't have very strong composition. The frame on the left is too full, and both have everything on one side of the frame. But put together (above), they make a picture with good balance.

Make the Photo

Here's how to take three shots that you can put together to make one spectacular view. First, choose a view that you like. Take three separate shots of it: one in the center, one where you are turned slightly left, and one where you are turned slightly right.

● Before you take your shots, move the camera around to make sure the picture will include everything you want to show.

● Try to include a little of the center view in both side views.

Once your photos are developed, put them together in a montage.

● Pictures in a montage can overlap.

● Don't worry if the top and bottom edges of the photos don't line up.

● Imagine what might be beyond the edges of the photos. You can extend the montage by drawing whatever you think will look good.

● Add cutouts from other photos if you like.

Picture Puzzle

Turn a photo panorama into a picture puzzle. It makes a great gift, and you can decide how easy or hard it will be to put back together.

You will need

- a piece of heavy white cardboard 27 cm x 50 cm (11 in. x 20 in.)
- a piece of corrugated cardboard (optional)
- a sheet of newspaper
- panorama photos from Make the Photo on page 19
- scissors, glue, colored pencils or markers, an X-Acto or utility knife
- picture cutouts or pieces of other photos

1 Lay the cardboard on the newspaper.

2 Line up your photos on the cardboard so that items in the photos are not repeated — you might have to trim them with scissors. Don't worry if the top and bottom edges of the pictures don't line up.

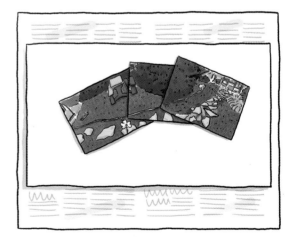

3 Glue the photos to the cardboard as you arranged them. Let dry.

4 Use colored pencils and markers to draw on the cardboard, adding to the scene. Add cutouts from other photos.

5 Turn the cardboard over and draw lines dividing it into pieces. The smaller the pieces, and the more the pieces are the same shape, the harder your puzzle will be.

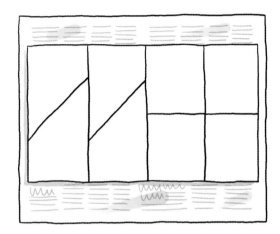

6 Ask an adult to help you cut the cardboard into pieces using the X-Acto knife. Cut on the corrugated cardboard to protect your work surface.

Eye Tricks

Photography is full of eye tricks. How can something big, like one of these kids, look so tiny in this photo? The farther things are in the background, the smaller they appear — that's called perspective.

 **Make the Photo**

Use perspective to create these fun optical illusions!

The Incredible Shrinking Friend

Have one friend stand in the foreground with one arm outstretched, and that hand open and flat. Send your second subject into the background. Look through the viewfinder and have the second subject move until he appears to be sitting on the hand of the person in the foreground. Then shoot!

Head in Hand

Find a corner of two walls. One should have a top wide enough to lie down on. Have one subject lie on the top of the wall on his back, with his feet facing the camera and arm out with palm facing up. His head should hang backwards over the far side of the wall. Have the other subject stand with his head in the hand of the first subject, and the rest of his body behind the wall.

● Take the photo straight on, so anything behind the wall doesn't show.

● Try this shot in sand or snow. Have the person whose head is showing lie on his stomach with arms and legs straight behind. Use the sand or snow to cover any parts of his body that are in view.

Action Shots

When you take a picture, you capture one moment in time. But you can show time passing by photographing something in motion. These are both pictures of the same pinwheel, but in the photo on the right, you know the pinwheel is moving because the colors are blending and show as a blur.

To take a picture like this, make sure that the camera shutter moves slowly — that way, anything moving faster than the shutter appears blurry. So even though your photo can't move, the viewer will see movement, as you see it here.

 **Make the Photo**

Try these action pictures to capture things on the move. Here are some tips to get you started:

● Steady yourself by standing firmly with your feet apart and your arms tight against your body. Use a tripod if you have one.

● Use film with a slow speed (200), and shoot on a cloudy day or in a darker room. This will force your shutter to move slowly to let in enough light for exposure.

Freaky Portrait

Have a friend quickly turn his head from side to side while you press the shutter release. If the camera shutter moves slowly enough, the photo will show the head as a blur or disappearing altogether, while the body remains in focus.

● Be as close as you can to your subject.

● To improve your chances of getting a good result, take two pictures.

● If you're not happy with the results, try again on a darker day or in a dark room, or try an even slower speed of film.

● In low light and with slow film, your shutter will move slowly to let in enough light, slowly enough to record the motion.

Riding Past

Have a friend ride past you on her bike or skateboard. Turn your body to follow her through the viewfinder as she passes. Practice a few times before you shoot, and then go for it. Snap the shutter as you follow your subject, and continue following her for a second after you release the shutter.

● Stand 4 m to 5 m (10 ft. to 15 ft.) from the subject.

● Take two pictures to improve your chances of getting a good result.

Summer Journal

Keep a photo journal of a vacation or field trip. Collect things you can use in your record of your holiday.

You will need

- photos taken while away
- souvenirs from the trip, such as postcards, ticket stubs, leaves and flowers
- pieces of construction paper, each 22 cm x 27 cm (8½ in. x 11 in.)
- 2 pieces of cardboard, each 23 cm x 30 cm (9 in. x 12 in.)
- scissors, a ruler, glue
- hole punch, yarn or string, colored pens, pencils or markers

1 Sort your photos and other items into groups. You can arrange them in chronological order, according to where they came from, or by type of souvenir.

2 Arrange the photos and souvenirs on construction paper, one page for each group. Trim or overlap the photos to make them fit better. Leave a 1 cm (½ in.) border on the left side of each journal page.

3 Glue everything down on the paper. Let dry.

4 Using colored pens, add captions to the pages, including when and where the photos were taken and other interesting information.

5 Measure and mark three holes along the left border of each page. Mark a hole in the center and one 5 cm (2 in.) up from the bottom and one 5 cm (2 in.) down from the top of the page. Punch holes at the marks.

6 Measure and mark three holes in each piece of cardboard. Along the 1 cm (½ in.) border, mark a hole in the center and one 6.5 cm (2½ in.) up from the bottom and one 6.5 cm (2½ in.) down from the top of the page. Carefully punch holes at the marks.

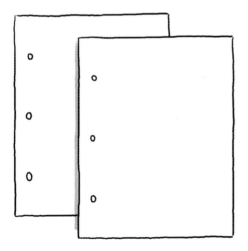

7 Put the journal pages between the two cardboard covers, lining up the holes. Use yarn or string to tie the journal together as shown.

8 Decorate the cover with a title, drawings, more photos and souvenirs.

Picturing People

When you take pictures of people, or portraits, you have a chance to show what a person is like. A portrait is not just a picture of someone, it is a picture about someone. Your photograph can show your subject's personality through lots of different clues — clothes, actions, expressions and gestures.

What can you tell about the boy in this picture? You can see that he is not afraid of the snake, and he is not shy with the person taking the picture. The plain background makes you focus on the person and not on where he is.

When you photograph people outside, the sun might make shadows on their faces, like in the photo on the left. Use the flash to fill in the shadows and you'll get a clear shot like the picture on the right.

☞ Try This

Wacky Portrait Puzzle

Take three photos of a person — one of the head and shoulders, then the body and finally the legs. The person can be in different poses for each shot, but take all three shots from about the same distance.

● You can try vertical shots (taller than they are wide), like these ones.

● Assemble the photos like puzzle pieces.

● You can overlap them so that parts of the body are not repeated.

● It's okay if the edges of the photos don't line up exactly.

📷 Make the Photo

Take before and after shots of a person. The "after" photo should be almost exactly the same as the first, but with one change. You could shoot a close-up of the face with eyes open and eyes closed, or with mouth relaxed and lips pursed in a kiss. How about before and after a haircut?

● Take both photos from the same distance.

● Make sure your subject fills the frame of each photo.

Before

and After

Here's a great way to use two pictures to show a before-and-after effect. When you look at the "picture accordion" from the left side, like the top photo, you get "before." When you look at it from the right side, like the bottom photo, you get "after." Use your portrait shots from page 29, or other pictures that show the same object changing over time.

You will need

- photos from Make the Photo on page 29
- a piece of cardboard 27 cm x 35 cm (11 in. x 14 in.)
- a pencil, a ruler, scissors, tape, glue

1 Using the pencil and ruler, divide each photo into four equal strips. On the back of the photos, number the strips from right to left: 1 to 4 for the before photo and 5 to 8 for the after.

2 Cut the photos into strips.

3 Arrange the strips, alternating them from each photo. The numbers should be in this order: 8, 4, 7, 3, 6, 2, 5, 1. (From the front, you see 1, 5, 2, 6, 3, 7, 4, 8.)

4 Tape the strips together along the back as shown. Fold the picture where the strips are joined.

| 8 | 4 | 7 | 3 | 6 | 2 | 5 | 1 |

5 Stand the joined picture up like an accordion. You should see the before photo when you look at it from the left, and the after photo when you look at it from the right.

6 Glue or tape the picture to the cardboard so it stays in the accordion shape.

Bird's-Eye View, Bug's-Eye View

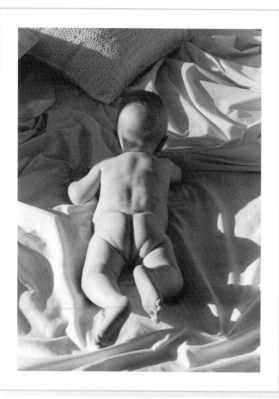

With photographs, you can make people see things in ways that they have never seen them before. You're used to looking at things head-on. Why not try a different point of view?

◀ This photo, taken from above the baby, could be any baby because you can't see the face. So its "babyness" is emphasized.

▼ A point of view below this seagull makes it look big and scary! Bird's-eye view, bug's-eye view — both give you a different look at the world.

Make the Photo

Stand on a chair to check out the way things look from up there. Now crawl around on your hands and knees to see things from below. Practice looking through the viewfinder of your camera this way. Plants might be boring if you look at them straight on, but they could look like a jungle from up close and down low.

Once you've looked at something from every angle, you're ready! Choose a subject and then shoot it from four different points of view.

▼ Get up high and shoot down at it.

● Move in tight and then back up far away — see how your subject looks different.

● Don't create a shadow by standing between the light and your subject.

▲ Shoot it from eye level, looking at it straight on.

▲ Get down low and shoot up at it.

▲ Shoot an abstraction that shows just part of the subject.

Step by Step

Every picture tells a story. When several pictures are arranged in an order that tells a story, it's called a sequence. Look at these pictures. Is it clear what is happening, and in what order? This sequence shows the story so clearly that it doesn't need captions, or words to go with the photos. Sometimes captions give the extra information viewers need to understand what they're looking at.

The exact number of photos needed to tell the story has been shown. Choosing photos like this is called editing. A good storyteller has to be a good editor.

Make the Photo

A map is like a story about the path you take to get somewhere. Plan and make a photo map that shows the way you get to school. Include the obvious landmarks — a store, a sign, even a crossing guard. Remember to include each change of direction. If you take a bus or get a ride, you could include where your best friend is picked up.

● Think about the viewer. Does your map have enough information for someone to follow your route?

● Try to use as few photos as are necessary to make a complete map.

Home

School

Connect the Shots

When you display your photos in an album or journal, they're connected in some way. A group of photos sharing a theme or idea is called a series.

A series is different from a sequence because pictures in a series can be viewed in any order.

It's easy to see the connection between these photos — they're all pictures of dogs! But they show different dogs in different poses, doing different things in different places. The photos in a series are connected, but it is the ways they differ that make a series interesting.

Make the Photo

Make a series of five photographs with a theme you know well — yourself. Include photos that will let your audience know you, like pictures of your favorite meal, your best friend or the place you go to be alone. Have someone take photos of you, or take photos yourself. A picture of yourself in the mirror is a picture of yourself as photographer!

▶ *I'm Alex, and this is my collection of Beanie Babies.*

▼ *My hands say a lot about me, because I use them to speak.*

▲ *Dressed up as a clown — but still me!*

▲ *I love rock climbing!*

◀ *I am signing "I love you" here.*

Tech Talk

If you photograph yourself in a mirror, your image might be out of focus. That's because your camera focused on the mirror, while your reflection was twice that distance away — from you to the mirror and back.

A-Day-in-the-Life Diorama

A diorama can be a 3-D version of a journal. It's a great way to display photographs and souvenirs from a special outing — or even just an ordinary day.

You will need

- a cereal box or shoebox
- decorating supplies, such as magazine cutouts, paints, fabric, sand, glitter, pebbles
- photos from Make the Photo on page 35 plus other photos
- pieces of cardboard
- things that tell about your day, such as toys, small objects, ticket stubs
- X-Acto knife; glue, glue stick or glue gun; scissors; a hole punch; thread, fishing line or string; tape

1 If you are using a cereal box, ask an adult to help you use the X-Acto knife to cut a window in one of the box's big sides.

2 Decorate the box with magazine cutouts, paint or fabric. You can glue on sand, glitter or pebbles.

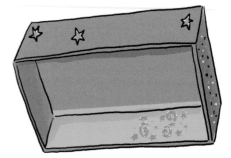

3 Arrange some of your photo map photos from page 35 on the inside of the box. Glue them down and let dry.

4 Arrange your other photos and objects in the box. Decide which items you want to hang from the "ceiling" of the box and which you want to stand on the "floor."

5 Crop the photos you want to hang or stand up. Glue them to pieces of cardboard. Let them dry and cut around the pictures with scissors.

6 Use the hole punch to make a hole at the top of each item you want to hang from the "ceiling" of your diorama. Tie one end of a piece of thread to each photo, and tape the other end to the inside top of the box.

7 To make photos stand on the bottom, or "floor," cut pieces of cardboard for tabs and glue them to the backs of the photos as shown. Let dry, fold up about 2 cm (1 in.), then glue or tape the tabs to the bottom of the box.

8 Glue paper objects, such as ticket stubs, to the inside of the box. Stand toys and other small objects inside.

Photographer Talk

abstraction: a picture that shows just part of a subject

aperture: the opening that lets light into the camera

background: the area of a photo that was far away from the camera

captions: words presented with photos to explain the photos

composition: the way a photo is planned — what is included and what is left out

crop: to cut away parts of the photo to show only what you want

digital camera: a camera that captures images in a digital file instead of on film

diorama: a three-dimensional display

diptych: a pair of pictures

editing: choosing photos for a sequence or series and deleting the ones not needed

film: a strip that has a coating on one side that is light-sensitive

foreground: the area of a photo that was close to the camera

lens: the piece of glass or plastic where the light collects to enter the camera

montage: several photos placed together

overexposed: when a photo is taken with too much light, making it pale and washed out

perspective: the way a distant object looks smaller than something the same size that is closer to the viewer

photogram: "writing with light" — an image made by light on paper instead of film

photography: "drawing with light" in ancient Greek — making images with a camera on light-sensitive film that is developed into pictures

pixels: "picture elements" — the pieces of information that make up a digital image

point of view: the angle you look at something from

portrait: a picture of a person (a picture you make of yourself is a self-portrait)

sequence: pictures arranged in order to tell a story

series: pictures that are connected in some way

shutter: a curtain inside the camera body that controls the light coming into the camera

shutter release: the button you push to take the picture

silhouette: the outside shape or outline of an object

subject: the thing or person you take a picture of

underexposed: when a photo is taken with too little light, making it too dark

viewfinder: the window in the camera that you look through